Connor Allen

Connor Allen is an award-winning multidisciplinary artist and former Children's Laureate of Wales (2021–2023). He holds an Honorary Doctorate in Literature from the University of South Wales.

Theatre credits include / Theatr yn cynnwys: Associate Artist at The Riverfront in Newport; performer with leading companies including National Theatre Wales, Taking Flight Theatre, Sherman Theatre, and the BBC. His acclaimed debut show *The Making of a Monster* premiered at Wales Millennium Centre in 2022 and won the Imison Award in 2023 for the radio version of the same name.

Television credits include / Teledu yn cynnwys: *The Outsiders*, *The Rapture*, and *Casualty*.

Writing credits include / Ysgrifennu yn cynnwys: *The Making of a Monster*; *Forgiveness of a Monster*; poetry collections *Dominoes and Miracles*.

A former member of the *BBC Welsh Voices, Welsh Royal Court Writers Group* and Hay Festival's *Writers at Work*, Connor's work explores themes of identity, masculinity, love, and grief.

First published in the UK in 2026 by Aurora Metro Publications Ltd

80 Hill Rise, Richmond, TW10 6UB

www.aurorametro.com   info@aurorametro.com

twitter @aurorametro FB/AuroraMetroBooks

Printed in the UK by 4edge Ltd. on sustainably resourced paper.

ISBN: 978-1-910798-13-3 (paperback)

ISBN: 978-1-910798-14-0 (e-book)

FORGIVENESS OF A MONSTER

BY

CONNOR ALLEN

AURORA METRO BOOKS

FORGIVENESS OF A MONSTER

CAST

Connor Allen
Mya Fox-Scott
Oraine Johnson

CREATIVE TEAM / TÎM CREADIGOL

Connor Allen	Writer / Awdur
Tonia Daley-Campbell	Director / Cyfarwyddwr
Ebrahim Nazier	Set and Costume Designer / Cynllunydd Set a Gwisgoedd
Laura Howard	Lighting Designer / Cynllunydd Goleuo
Oraine Johnson	Composer and Sound Designer / Cyfansoddwr a Cynllunydd Sain
Orique Johnson	Second Sound Designer / Ail Cynllunydd Sain
Tia-zakura Camilleri	Assistant Director / Cyfarwyddwr Cynorthwyol
Gemma Boaden	Voice Director / Cyfarwyddwr Llais
Jodi Ann Nicholson	Movement Director / Cyfarwyddwr Symudiad
Ndidi John	Wellbeing Facilitator / Hyfforddwr Lles
Davina Moss, Lowri Morgan	Dramaturgy
Branwen Davies	Additional Dramaturg / Dramaturg Ychwanegol

PRODUCTION TEAM / TÎM CYNHYRCHU

Mandy Ivory-Castile	Production Manager / Rheolwr Cynhyrchu
Rachel Mortimer	Technical Manager / Rheolwr Technegol
Josh Miles	Company Stage Manager / Rheolwr Llwyfan y Cwmni
Amy Clarke	Deputy Stage Manager / Dirprwy Reolwr Llwyfan
Elizabeth Welsh	Assistant Stage Manager / Rheolwr Llwyfan Cynorthwyol
Charlie Moore	LX Programmer / Rhaglennydd LX
Ruby James, Emily Howard	Technicians / Technegwyr
Kate Turton	Costume Supervisor / Goruchwyliwr Gwisgoedd
Matt Carter	Workshop Manager / Rheolwr Gweithdy
Matt Cartner, Archie Adams, Edward Selwood, Will Hawkins	Construction / Adeiladwaith
Emily Jones, Kayleigh Smith	Scenic Artists / Artistiaid Golygfaol

Julia Barry
Chief Executive / Prif Weithredwr

Francesca Goodridge
Artistic Director / Cyfarwyddwr Artistig

CARDIFF'S THEATRE FOR WALES

Imagine a world made more equitable, more compassionate, more unified by the power of theatre. We are driven to achieve this vision every day. We do this by creating and curating shared live theatre experiences that inspire people from all backgrounds across South Wales to make a better world, in their own way. We believe that access to creativity and self-expression is a right and we constantly strive to ensure everyone has the opportunity to be enriched by the art of theatre.

Our focus on the development and production of new writing and on nurturing Welsh and Wales-based artists makes us the engine room of Welsh theatre. We tell Welsh stories with global resonance through our Made at Sherman productions, created under our roof right here in the heart of Cardiff. We're a place for everyone, generating opportunities for the citizens of South Wales to connect with theatre through inspiring and visionary engagement.

THEATR I GYMRU YNG NGHAERDYDD

Dychmygwch fyd lle gall pŵer y theatr greu byd tecach, mwy tosturiol ac unedig. Cawn ein hysgogi i gyflawni'r weledigaeth yma yn ddyddiol. Rydyn ni'n gwneud hyn drwy greu a churadu profiadau theatr byw i'w rhannu ac i ysbrydoli pobl o bob cefndir ar draws De Cymru i fedru gwneud byd gwell, yn eu ffordd eu hunain. Credwn fod pawb â'r hawl i gael mynediad at greadigrwydd a hunanfynegiant, ac ymdrechwn yn gyson i sicrhau bod pawb yn cael y cyfle i gael eu cyfoethogi gan y theatr.

Mae ein ffocws ar ddatblygu a chynhyrchu gwaith newydd ac ar feithrin artistiaid Cymraeg ac o Gymru yn ein gwneud ni'n injan i fyd y theatr yng Nghymru. Trwy ein cynyrchiadau Crëwyd yn y Sherman, rydym yn adrodd straeon Cymraeg sy'n cyseinio negeseuon o bwys yn fyd-eang, a chaiff pob un eu creu o dan ein to yng nghalon Caerdydd. Rydym yn le i bawb, gan greu cyfleoedd i bobl De Cymru gysylltu â'r theatr drwy ymrwymiad ysbrydoledig a gweledigaethol.

SHERMAN THEATRE IS A REGISTERED CHARITY.
Donate today to help to secure our future.

MAE THEATR Y SHERMAN YN ELUSEN GOFRESTREDIG.
Cyfrannwch heddiw i helpu i sicrhau ein dyfodol.

SHERMANTHEATRE.CO.UK

Sherman Cymru Productions Ltd | Registered Charity Number / Rhif Elusen Cofrestredig 1118364

BIOGRAPHIES / BYWGRAFFIADAU

Mya Fox-Scott – Performer / Perfformiwr

Theatre credits include / Theatr yn cynnwys: *Mama Goose* (Stratford East); *Sleeping Beauty* (New Wolsey Theatre); *Welfare* (Derby Theatre); *Standing at the Sky's Edge* (Gillian Lynne Theatre, West End); *Peter Pan* (Little Wolf Entertainment); *Curtains, Julius Caesar, A Funny Thing Happened on the Way to the Forum, A School for Scandal, Sweat, Paradise* (Royal Central School of Speech and Drama); *Emma Rice Wise Children Workshop* (Wise Children).

Oraine Johnson – Performer, Composer and Sound Designer / Perfformiwr, Cyfansoddwr a Cynllunydd Sain

Theatre credits include / Theatr yn cynnwys: *Grease The Musical* (Blackpool Grand); *The Great Gatsby* (Pitlochry Theatre); *Jungle Book, Robin Hood* (Derby Theatre); *One Man, Two Guv'nors* (Queens Theatre); *One Flew Over the Cuckoo's Nest* (Torch Theatre); *Hallowed Turf* (Eden Court Theatre); *Sorry! No Coloureds, No Irish, No Dogs* (Arena Theatre); *Tin Violin* (Minack Theatre); *Of Mice and Men* (Lowry Theatre).

Film and Television credits include / Ffilm a Teledu yn cynnwys: *Domino Effect* (Apple TV); *Choice* (C4); *Repercussions* (Wandering Tiger); *World Cup* (Sony Entertainment Channel); *Lynx Rally* (MTV). Composing credits include / Cyfansoddi yn cynnwys: producing and creating music for both National and regional theatres, most recently for *Dr Jekyll and Hyde* (Royal Derngate); *Lucid The Dreamwalker Audiobook* (published by Gollancz); *Wanted* (National Tour); *My Grandparents and I* (Sudden Productions at Midland Arts Centre); *The Making of a Monster* (Wales Millennium Centre / Canolfan Mileniwm Cymru).

Oraine is a multi-disciplined actor/musician/singer who has performed at the O2 Indigo London, NEC and produced for various artists; airing original music on BBC Radio 1, 1xtra and other mainstream stations. Oraine has also found success as an author. His first book from his trilogy *Lucid The Dreamwalker* was recently commercially published worldwide by Gollancz publishing house.

Tonia Daley-Campbell – Director / Cyfarwyddwr

Tonia Daley-Campbell is a hyphenated creative. A director, actor, award-winning writer, published author, host and creative consultant. She has been working in the creative industries for 30 years and has recently taken up a position at The Wolverhampton Grand Theatre as the new Head of Audiences and Creative. In 2022 Tonia was nominated for a Black British Theatre award for her pioneering work in theatre. Tonia is an energetic whirlwind of creative energy, she creates open safe spaces for creatives to be inspired and thrive.

Ebrahim Nazier – Set and Costume Designer / Cynllunydd Set a Gwisgoedd

Ebrahim Nazier is a set and installation designer, musician, filmmaker and seamster who makes spaces that enhance the places they inhabit.

Design and artist work includes / Gwaith dylunio ac artistiaid yn cynnwys: work with Friction Arts, Cloud Cuckoo Land, The RSC, The Legacy Centre, Fox Rocha, BOA Stage and Screen, Ad Infinitum, Natalie Mason, Lynnebec and Artists On The Edge. From 2015-2021, he held posts as Head of Technical Design and Head of Workshops at the Birmingham REP Theatre where he designed technical structures for a multitude of productions including *One Love: The Bob Marley Musical, Nativity! The Musical* and *What Shadows*. He also designed sets for REP productions *GrimeBoy, Scenes from a Brummie Iliad, Sky Comedy Rep* and *Foundry Festival*.

As an Architectural Technologist / Fel Tech-nolegydd Pensaernïol: Ebrahim spent a decade working in commercial, industrial and residential architecture in Cape Town, London and Birmingham. His expertise in spatial design and construction remains with him across disciplines in his theatre and installation work.

Laura Howard – Lighting Designer / Cynllunydd Goleuo

Theatre credits include / Theatr yn cynnwys: *The Memory of Water* (Bolton Octagon / Liverpool Everyman & Playhouse); *Safe Space* (Chichester Festival Theatre); *Snake in the Grass* (Theatr Clwyd); *Elephant* (Menier Chocolate Factory); *Millennium Girls* (Brixton House); *Takeaway, The Lieutenant of Inishmore, The Legend of Ned Ludd* (Liverpool Everyman); *The Habits* (Hampstead Theatre); *Lavender, Hyacinth, Violet, Yew, This Might Not Be It, Elephant, The Kola Nut Does Not Speak English, Clutch, Invisible* (Bush Theatre); *Mr Snow* (Leeds Playhouse); *Santi & Naz* (UK tour / Taith DU / The Thelmas); *Work It Out* (HOME); *The Good John Proctor, Odyssey: A Heroic Pantomime* (Jermyn Street Theatre); *Snow Queen* (Polka Theatre); *Black Is...* (New Diorama / Company Three); *Brassic FM* (Gate Theatre); *Salty Irina* (Roundabout Paines Plough); *Dismissed, Splintered, Juniper and Jules* (Soho Theatre); *Faun* (UK tour / Taith DU / Cardboard Citizens); *I Hate It Here* (Pleasance Theatre); *The Beach House* (Park Theatre); *Manorism* (Southbank Centre); *Exodus* (National Theatre of Scotland); *Dead Air* (Stockroom / Riverside Studios); *I Hate It Here* (Camden People's Theatre); *Moreno* (Theatre 503); *Cells Out* (Camden People's Theatre / Glasshouse Theatre).

Tia-zakura Camilleri – Assistant Director / Cyfarwyddwr Cynorthwyol (role supported by the / rôl a gefnogir gan y Loyalty Programme)

Tia-zakura is a published writer, theatre-maker and spoken-word poet from Cardiff who blends rhythm, wordplay and music, captivating audiences on iconic stages including the Southbank Centre, Roundhouse and the Jazz Cafe.

Theatre includes / Theatr yn cynnwys: Tia has trained and assisted on productions with Welsh National Opera, Music Theatre Wales and the Jerwood Trainee Director Programme at the Young Vic.

Playwriting includes / Ysgrifennu dramâu yn cynnwys: her debut, *Girl-Coded*, a spoken-word theatre production, opened at Wales Millennium Centre in April 2026. Tia also won a Royal Television Society Wales Award for her short documentary, *Ya Bilaadi*.

Jodi Ann Nicholson – Movement Director / Cyfarwyddwr Symudiad

Jodi Ann Nicholson is a South Wales based inter-disciplinary movement artist and director. Her practice spans contemporary performance, theatre, and live work, with a focus on how movement can deepen narrative, character, and emotional landscape.

She works collaboratively with performers and creative teams to develop a physical language that supports storytelling, drawing on improvisation, embodiment, and lived experience. She has a particular sensitivity when working with autobiographical material, creating supportive, considered processes that allow personal narratives to be explored with care and agency.

Jodi's work spans theatre, outdoor performance, and interdisciplinary contexts, including *Fabulous Animals* (2023) and *Happinessless* R&D (2022). Alongside her movement direction, she develops her own performance work, including her solo project *Dear, Love From...*

Connor Allen. Photo: Chillee Noir, 2026.

AUTHOR'S NOTE

To David,

Thank you

For saving my life

When I first started on this journey of making work and telling a story, never in my wildest dreams did I think this chopsy kid from Hammond Drive would have a published play, LET ALONE TWO!

But here I am still, as proof that stories and experiences matter. They guide us through life and through a world that can feel busy, loud, and overwhelming at times.

As a child of two cultures and two worlds, I grew up existing in a grey area, never quite feeling black enough or white enough. Not knowing where I fitted in and that confusion led to rage and hurt in my teenage years. The older I have gotten, the more I have understood that anger is just fear in disguise, and the more I look at the choices I made and the journey I have been on, the more I have understood that fear was at the root of it all. But it's okay to be scared; that's human.

We're multi-faceted beings. Complex and contradictory at times. There's something powerful in accepting that. In embracing the duality within us. Your twenties, at least for me, have been about figuring out who you are. It's not been a straight road, but it's been a necessary one.

They say you don't always realise you've been on a journey until you pause, look back, and see all the footprints that led you to where you are now. 'Forgiveness' is me sharing some of those footprints that I have reflected on, the questions I've wrestled with, and the steps that have brought me here. I have to shout out Davina for seeing value in my footprints and pushing me to tell this story. I hope and pray that it can help and be a way of navigating tough times and questions that others have because I know I'm not the only one feeling this way.

Life is fragile. Being human is hard. In a world that demands perfection, we are conditioned to hide our wounds and present something that's polished and not always the truth. Especially as men, because we don't talk. And in that lies the problem! I have lost too many people in my life because they didn't feel like they could talk! Someone wise told me that if I heal, then we all heal, as I'll learn some stuff that I can share and pass on, and that ripple effect allows others to see themselves.

I have so many people to thank for continuously supporting me and being a part of my story and journey. You know who you are! And just know I love you all. You are all ingredients in the recipe that is this story.

To my father and my mum...

Thank you for being human. And walking a journey that led to me.

To Branwen, there is no universe of stories, no *Monster*, no Connor the writer without you, so thank you for having my back and keeping it real through the ups and downs and guiding a lost soul at times.

To Amie, thank you for truly showing me the man I want to be and having patience as I figured and am still figuring that out. You're my diamond.

To Blade, thank you for being my strength and colour. You are the strongest man I know and a constant motivation to be better.

To Chloe, I hope I made you proud.

To Jodi... thank you for being my Pops when I needed that comfort and guidance. I love you.

FORGIVENESS OF A MONSTER

by

Connor Allen

CHARACTERS

CONNOR
CONNOR, aged 10
LITTLE BLACK BOY
THE VOID
FATHER
THE THERAPIST
THE ANGEL
LUCY
BUTTERFLIES
MUM
BLADE
LOCAL
THE MUSICIAN (ORAINE)

Forgiveness of a Monster was first performed on 8 May 2026 at Sherman Theatre.

Perfformiwyd *Forgiveness of a Monster* am y tro cyntaf ar 8 Mai 2026 yn Theatr y Sherman.

CONTENTS

*What Do I See *and* Father Time *lyrics were co-written with Tia-zakura Camilleri & Mace The Great.*

The doors are the gateways to the story

The stage is black. A void. Nothing can be seen.

Butterflies are flying around. Sound of wings. Glitches can be heard.

We are inside Connor's mind.

Connor's voice can be heard saying the following as the audience enter.

Lord forgive me for all my sins

I don't know if I believe in God

But I believe in external force

Fragments of Connor's mind can be heard building and building towards a crescendo.

Different voices. Different memories. Different times.

All playing out.

Voicenotes on repeat such as "How do I get past myself?" "Do I have anger in my DNA?"

George Floyd yelling out, Dr Who and the TARDIS echoing out, Power Rangers morphing and Spider-Man webbing.

Different chapters and nostalgia building and overlapping A symphony of thoughts and memories.

Building

and

Building

and

Building.

Voice of Connor's mum rings out.

MUM   Because son you look exhausted. You can't keep burning the candle at both ends. You really need some therapy or something.

CONNOR   Be serious Mum I ain't doing therapy, real men don't go therapy.

MUM   I'm worried about you.

Glitch.

Lucy is sat crossed legged in a dimly lit smoke filled dimension.

She is looking through an ancient book with different artefacts surrounding her. Incantations/phrases are being spoken and she is mixing together a concoction. A photo of Connor is front and centre among the artefacts.

Lucy is singing incantations.

LUCY   Death approaches
                It catches us all
                A soul for a soul
                And now an angel falls

                A deal made on a beach
                To protect a child's heart
                Decades of manipulation
                Tore many souls apart

                To keep me rejuvenated
                A new deal must be made
                A continuation of a legacy
                So there's no soul to save

> I'm coming for you Connor
> Your soul will be mine
> Tick tock tick tock
> You're running out of time

Darkness remains.

Glitch.

The voice of The Therapist rings out in the void. Churchill Downs instrumental starts to fill the space.

SEEING

THE THERAPIST *(V.O)* Monday 7th February 2022.

> I'm sat here with Connor.
>
> This is our first session.
>
> And we're just going to talk about you.
>
> Your background.
>
> Where you're from.
>
> Who are you?
>
> Any issues you've been dealing with.
>
> So Connor, where shall we start...

One single spotlight dimly shines down and reveals Connor in the middle of the void. Smoke is brimming on the surface.

All we see is him.

CONNOR   Look...

> Where do I start?
>
> Like really where do I start
>
> Last few years I've been feeling like Usain Bolt
>
> Running and running so fast
>
> On the one hand my career is gaining ground
>
> On the other my personal life feels like I drowned
>
> There's stress
>
> There's sex
>
> My need to be the best

A distraction from the struggles inside
my head
Do you ever just look in the mirror
Wonder who or what is looking back at you?
Cos I do

Some days you got it all together
Other days you haven't got no clue

But you asked who are you?

So, who am I?   I can't lie
I don't even know who am I?

It's more complex than just
my name is Connor and I'm approaching 30
So let me take you on a journey
Straight into my past

From a young age
Humour and rage
The reality of the estate
Age 11
Best friend Lloyd died of a brain tumour
Survivors guilt as he never lived out his
future
But I'm living out mine
His mum gave me his watch
A reminder

As the most precious thing is time

Fast forward through my teenage years the numerous
comments of you're not really mixed race
Are you?
You're the same colour as me

Too white for the Blacks
Too Black for the whites
I'm exhausted
Sick and tired of having to fight
To exist as a mixed race kid
Suppress my anger so I don't blow my lid
Like I did in 07
When I hit my mum
Ever since then I been on the run
Decades long Atonement
For the shame of that moment

Even though my mum forgave me for what
I did to her
It still haunts me after all these years

Looking back at that chapter of my life
Was told I'd be in prison or at the end of
a knife
Either way two women believed in me
Believed I could be anything I wanted to be

Mum and nan
Knew I was so much more than the "Angry
Black Man"

With Welsh and Jamaican flowing through
my veins
My light skin is the stem of most of my
pains
From both sides no acceptance lots of
disdain
Like a storm with no light after the rain

See I'm just a mixed race kid from a council
estate
Navigating a world of so much hate
But do I contribute with the actions I use
Or am I simply being obtuse

Cos all I see is grey
Not black and white
In the world there's good and evil
Where Hurt people hurt people
But is that a rule for humanity
Or what I use to justify the man in me

Like "Toxic Masculinity"

Men that I look up to hiding all their cries
Cos they don't wanna be pussy
they don't wanna be weak

So they don't let no salt fall onto their
cheeks
Men programmed to not show feelings
Being sensitive is too revealing

So we bottle up
Don't open up
Feels like I'm gunna explode
time to unload
Finally the pressure's too much

See I grew up a fatherless child
And all the trauma of that
Is masked through smiles

But the older I'm getting
I'm realising I ain't smiled in a while

See, lately I've been through a lot
Got me questioning am I still me
Maybe I'm not
Am I a fake, am I fraud?
                    Chasing the applause
Chasing all my dreams
But the reality I am in is not what it seems

Approaching the next chapter of 30s
All this shit has caught up with me
There's problem after problem

> Buried inside my head
> I need to address it before I take my life
> Just like my cousin did
> And suddenly I'm dead/

A glitch happens and a different memory is bleeding through Distortion.

Lucy emerges out of the shadows to comfort Connor.

LUCY   There there child.

It's okay.

Lucy is here.

You've been through so much.

Pain and loss.

You're hurting. I can see that.

Been hurting for so so long.

Let me help you.

Stop the hurt.

Connor contemplates.

Look, nothing is set in stone right now. Here's my card.

Connor takes the card.

I won't abandon you.

As he does the lights snap open on a grave.

We see smoke filling the brim of the surface and dirt/soil covering the depths of the void.

He is visibly shook like he doesn't quite know where he is for a second. The Therapist's voice echoes out like he is calling to Connor.

THE THERAPIST   Connor are you paying attention?
Stop moving around the edges and let's get to the heart of it.

CONNOR   I'm busy a sec.

Glitch.

Connor notices the audience.

CONNOR   That was weird.
Super weird.
I was just (somewhere else).

Strange where your mind takes you when you're inside your head.
Alone with your thoughts.

Hi, Sorry.

I should probably start with...
I'm Connor.
Thank you all for coming, to my fortress of solitude.

Apologies for being late.
I used to blame it on 'Black man timing'.
Like that's a real thing. I kid you not.
But then I was like I can only really blame half my timekeeping on it as I'm only half Black y'know.
Half Jamaican to be specific. That's where all this came from.

Connor looks at the grave and the surroundings.

This whole thing. Generations upon generations. See, in Caribbean culture, primarily Jamaica, there's a thing called nine night.

Originating from the Ashanti people of west Africa.

Modern day Ghana for those who are interested.

And then adopted by many Caribbean islands.

Basically when someone one passes, people will gather in their 'yard' (home) to celebrate the life that was lived for nine days and nine nights with stories of life and triumphs, fondest memories, songs and lots of drinking. Can't forget the drinking.

Connor offers some rum out to the audience. A butterfly flies past. He ignores it and picks an audience member as he's handing out rum. He gets to know them and does a short improvisation around what they think Forgiveness is to them? What does it mean?

He repeats it a few times.

Total honesty I'm still figuring out what it means.

They say anger and resentment only hurts the person that's carrying it.

I couldn't agree more.

I used to think forgiveness was this one way road. Like it came from the person you've done wrong, right?

It's not. It's a two way street.

He makes a toast

So let's make a toast.

To the versions of us we see in the mirror and to the stories that have made us who we are. We honour you.

Connor drinks and then pours a little rum into the grave as he does his phone rings. He sends it to voicemail.

CONNOR   That's a point. Is everyone's phone on silent?

I know you're probably thinking whose grave is that.

I think it's easier if I just show you how I got here.

Because it's all interconnected.

But I'll need to go right back to the beginning.

Not of my story.

But of a little child in Jamaica.

The Angel climbs out of the grave.

THE ANGEL   And it's not just a story of generational history, but one about legacy too.

Connor looks in the mirror, the doorway, and sees a little black child on a beach staring out at a boat.

CONNOR   I see you.

ONCE UPON A TIME

As Connor walks through the mirror, sounds of time reversing are echoing out. The Angel goes over to the mic. A Tems-inspired instrumental kicks in.

She starts a story.

THE ANGEL   Once upon a time
In a country so Devine
In the West Indies
Called Jamaica
It was fine
1948
People looked for an escape

One day
their wish was granted
Cos on the other side of the pond
The UK was recovering from war
and getting bombed
So to help rebuild
They welcomed an influx
on board HMS Windrush
Hundreds upon hundreds
of people
left over the decades that passed
To forge a better future
Their own everlast

Fast forward
You're 9 years old
clinging to the promises
that you were told
As you watch your parents
sail off into the sunset
Leaving you with a hole in your heart
As they depart
You're left with your nan
Deep regret
Questioning
Why aren't I enough?
Why have I got to stay and they got to go?
Lord knows
On that sandy beach in St Elizabeth
You decide
You're not going to feel this way
You're not gunna let the insecurities
have their say
You make a deal with this mysterious figure
Called Lucy
To sell part of your soul to fill the absent hole
Who knew the powers of juju
Would split you in two
Reincarnation rebuilt brand new

She gives you the power
to never feel pain like this again
You'll have charm and charisma x10

To use and manipulate

Over the years

Fill the absent hole

So the scars won't show

you stay on that

tiny island

You stay with your nan

To raise you to become a man/

We see a little Black boy in the mirror with the ocean behind him and the sand beneath his feet.

Glitch.

A piece of poetry is bled through the mirror recited by Connor.

(V.O) ***So... how do I sum this up***

When all I had

Was my mothers love

We hear the therapist's voice echoing through the mirror as the image of the boy disappears.

THE THERAPIST The date is Monday 11th April 2022.

I'm sat here with Connor.

It's our 4th session. Following on from our last session.

We are just going to explore further the issues raised about your background, your heritage and your father.

So where shall we start...

WHAT WOULD YOU/I SAY?

Connor walks through into the therapy room. Two seats are opposite each other. One has a microphone on it. The mic is Connor's therapy sessions. He spits his truth.

The voice recording plays until Connor is in the chair. Recording stops and in to the scene.

CONNOR   Dunno where to start. Ain't it your job to lead?

THE THERAPIST Well, how are you feeling in yourself? In regards to what's been going on.

CONNOR   Dark thoughts about a world without me in it.

One minute I'm happy.

Then I'm back to being angry and sad again.

THE THERAPIST Focusing in on what your ex said. That you're just like your father.

CONNOR   I fucking hate that. I'm nothing like him

He abandoned his kids, had multiple lives.

Beat.

She said I had 2 different personas.

Maybe she was right.

Like a classic Gemini.

I got the angel and the devil conversing on both shoulders.

THE THERAPIST What do they say?

CONNOR   Just at war with each other.

Constantly.

> One trying to sway me away from evil and the other leading me to temptation.

Beat.

THE THERAPIST So you want to be nothing like your dad/

CONNOR /Father!

And I AM nothing like him

THE THERAPIST Okay. So do you want to BE a dad?

CONNOR I did. Not quite sure anymore.

THE THERAPIST Well, who you choose to have kids with is one of the most important decisions of one's life.

CONNOR Then why the fuck did my mum choose him?

Not once, not twice but three times.

Even after they lost a child.

Like c'mon.

THE THERAPIST Children connect parents. For life. Especially ones that are taken too soon.

What can you tell me about your sister?

CONNOR Dunno. I wasn't born. She passed in 91.

I was born in 92.

All I know is that her dying messed them up.

THE THERAPIST Well...

Maybe your father is your mother's only connection to her. And vice versa.

Connected forever.

What would you say to him? If he was here?

CONNOR Dunno.

Fuck all because he's not.

THE THERAPIST Right, but what would you say?

Got lots to say Connor and you can articulate it in a way that others can't.

So what would you say?

CONNOR This is dumb.

THE THERAPIST Stop deflecting and avoiding answering.

Awkward pause.

What would you say to him?

All this anger. All these questions. What would you say?

A butterfly passes by and Connor notices it for the first time.

He touches the glass and as he does he hears Michael Jackson's 'Butterflies' playing through a different mirror.

He is drawn in and enters the mirror to the memory.

Connor travels through the mirror fully and is back in his bedroom at 10 years old.

As he is passing through the mirror Connor's phone rings – it's his mum. He ignores it.

CONNOR Dear Santa,

I know you're a busy man.

So I'll keep this brief.

As you're probably aware through your naughty and nice list, I have been super good this year.

You can even ask my mum. She'll vouch for me.

And I know initially sent you my Christmas list and the main two things I wanted were the red power ranger costume and a gameboy colour with mario 6 golden coins to go with it.

But lately I have been thinking and I have seen what you did to Micheal Jackson making him black to white so I was wondering if you could do the reverse to me. Make me darker.

Then I could be closer to my father.

So if you could make that happen, I'd be super grateful.

And I promise to keep on being good.

Thank you Santa.

Connor Allen, aged 10.

And I stick it in an envelope.
Write:
To Santa Claus
The North Pole
With no postcode
though as
postmen know
where Santa
lives.
It's Santa after all.
Give it to my mum to take to the postbox.
As I put on my socks and trainers

go out and play with friends
endless fun building dens
playing gang-tag
freedom in the estate.
Happiness and laughter.
But none from mum as she reads the letter.
And lacks any power to make her son better.
So Mum sits me down
tries to explain that I am perfect just the
way I am. But can't explain why I am light
skinned and my little brother Blade is
brown.
You see that's confusing.
Too white for my black friends and family.
Too black for my white friends and family.

Where do I fit in?

I'm only half of one and half of the other.
And I'm constantly reminded of that.

My story is a complex Thriller
Intertwined History
None the less
Between 2 countries
2 cultures
But I must confess devastation
at never being understood
From a fresh page at a young age
No one understanding how I felt

Made me want to Fly Away
Made me Scream
Inward in my mind
Outward at the world

I can't be the only one feeling this way
Just wanting a father

To show up and stay
To hold me and just say
son you are not alone
This eruption of emotion
confusion of sense

It's human nature
It's okay
Whatever happens
I'll be there
But I didn't get that

I got absence
Unanswered questions

See, I remember the time
Being torn from a young age
Confusion of identity
Black and white
Anger and rage
It's dangerous

Flying off the rails
Flying off the wall
People writing me off
As a trouble maker
That bad kid
Just wanting the pain to stop
wanting to be free
wanting to be me
But no tools to regulate
The emotional waves inside crashing
Like butterflies
flapping and flapping
Like it's going to destroy you from within

I look
I don't see a man in the mirror
I see a child

Connor looks at the mirror and sees the same little Black boy from before on the beach.

THE THERAPIST What would you say to the child?

Connor picks up the microphone and starts to spit as Pepper Riddim creeps in. The mic is his therapist. Here he is fully raw and vulnerable.

WHAT WOULD I SAY?

CONNOR   What would I say?

THE THERAPIST What would you say?

CONNOR   What would I say?

Yo, what would I say?
What would I say
To a wasteman that was never around
Always out there acting a clown
You are the talk of Newport town
With all your Multiple women
And all those Multiple kids
What? Man are you taking the piss
Whatever happened to taking me to feed
those ducks
I know you didn't give a fuck
so

Fuck you and your Broken Promises
Fuck you and your Dead chess moves
Fuck you for never having a clue
about all the shit you put me through
Cos you're just a serial offender
man's got no agenda
Just out there abusing different women
you're a herald of lucifer
you just keep on sinnin'

How many lives you fucked now
you lost count
how many kids you got now?
you lost count
how many hearts you broke now?
you lost count

Yeah it's alright I'll remind you
Cos the number it's around 42
And woooo

What you gunna do
About your dick?
You gunna start wrapping
Or just keep on stacking
Kid after kid
Do you even remember

The names of the ones you hid
Man you're taking the piss
Bro's just taking the piss

Where was you when I needed you
That's right
You weren't around
If I wanted to call you dad
It was never allowed
Where was you
during my first heartbreak
I can't fake the emotions that I felt
It was like when I was naughty and you'd
take off your belt
You would
beat me black and blue
I didn't care cos it meant
I got to spend more time with you/

Connor freezes as the music continues until the therapist interjects.

THE THERAPIST So it's safe to say you carry some resentment? Some pain?

Is that fair to say?

CONNOR I think that's enough for today.

Connor puts the mic down and exits through the mirror into the void.

Visibly upset, he takes out Lucy's card from the beginning and contemplates ringing it. Unaware that Lucy is already lurking in the void waiting to pounce.

THE OFFER

LUCY Connor...

Connor jumps

CONNOR I was just about to/

LUCY /What's wrong Con?

I can call you Con, right?

CONNOR I've been thinking. I uh/

LUCY /You do poetry, yeah?

Roses are Red

Violets are Blue

My name's Lucy

I won't abandon you

Laughs hysterically.

C'mon

I thought you was keeping it gangsta

Or womaniser

Stone hearted

Different womens beds
Getting all the head
I thought you was on a fuck-the-world
attitude

I don't wanna intrude
On your little therapy sessions

But court
Is
In
Session

My name is Lucy, Connor
You know I want you, Connor

Lucy can calm that mess
That's right up there inside your head

Lucy just wants your trust and Loyalty
She wants you to see
How powerful you could really be

Lucy just wants to push you harder
She knows how much you hate your father

Lucy's not shy
She's just out here looking for the right guy

That guy is you
Connor
Now you're at that age
Where you're conflicted
You can sign this contract
And everything is possible
Sign this contract and you'll truly be
Unstoppable

Connor contemplates it for a second before the void glitches and we are back in the present, back with the audience. He goes over to the bookshelf of the void and pulls out a giant pop-up book of Mary Shelley's Frankenstein.

CONNOR   Do you ever think parents look at their creations with shame or regret?

To create life is a Godlike power but to abandon your creation... What does that say?

My nan, 'great woman', said we are all built on stories. So here's one. On what it means to be human.

It's of a man. Obsessed with leaving his mark on the world. Obsessed with death in some complicated way, he creates life, one of the most powerful things humanly possible.

He's a God in that sense.

But the moment that life comes into the world, he rejects it. Abandons his creation. Refuses to nurture it or empathise with the situation he has placed his creation in.

Now the creation, this creature of some sorts, starts off innocent, a child longing for connection with his creator, but repeatedly rejected over the years, he then becomes consumed by abandonment and rage. Not a great combination, trust me I should know.

He lashes out on those closest to him committing acts of violence which his creator is disgusted by and angry with of course.

Years later when the man dies, his creation shows up mourning his creator and showing remorse for his violent actions of the past.

So... who is really to blame – the one who commits violent acts, or the one who created and abandoned him?

I sometimes look at my creator.

Leaving me with this Blackness, this racialised identity but with no tools on how to deal or navigate that.

No help on how to deal with the racism and micro-aggressions.

No help on how to care for and look after my afro hair which looks dry and out of place.

No nurturing or empathy.

Just absence.

He just saw a monster.

Connor gets a text.

CONNOR   Sorry.

Mum again.

Text is shown projected:

'Connor ring me when you're not busy. Need to talk to you.'

It's funny because you know what people would see when I was younger? And even now to some degree.

Only half of me.

See I'm a 90s baby.

And once upon a time

Half Caste was the term that was used.

I went through life not having the tools to combat the ignorance. I took it upon myself to learn what things mean.

Has anyone heard of the term Half Caste before? Show of hands?

Okay... Does anyone know it's origins?

Half Caste.

Comes from latin word 'Castus' which means clean or pure. So add on the half and the term means half pure.

Or impure.

Purity equals white so being half white or half pure just dirties the blood as some so eloquently put it.

> There's power in learning the meaning behind things.

The therapist interjects. His voice can be heard like a voice recording through a mirror.

THE THERAPIST   Connor, who are you talking to?

Beat.

> Why are you always performing?

Connor walks through the mirror into Therapy. The Angel appears.

THE ANGEL   Like a guardian angel on his shoulder, I've watched all his chapters.

> Just want him to get his happy ever after.
>
> Because I've seen it all.
>
> His highs his lows.
>
> Even there when he came to blows.
>
> With teachers, his exes, even his mum.

Connor is a distant shadow in the mirror. The angel watches him.

> I see a big heart that's desperate to love and also be loved in return.
>
> I see a man who tortures himself for past mistakes.
>
> I see a caterpillar longing to become a butterfly.
>
> I see a story.
>
> That started way before him.
>
> Long before me even.
>
> With a little child in Jamaica/

The Angel stands there in the centre.

*The same Tems-inspired instrumental from earlier kicks
in as The Angel approaches a microphone and continues
the story she was telling.*

Fast forward

Years and years pass

The abuse of power

gets bolder and bolder

You're a master of the black magic

The juju is coursing

straight through you

The list of women

It's more than just a few

You're racking up a tally

Walking around with a metaphorical bally

And all the pain you ran from

Is numbed

By money and sex

This feeling is nothing like the rest

Now you're a man so

You leave your nan

You pay to travel to the UK

You're different

You're grown

Confidence instilled to make it on your
own

In the UK

People look at you different

But one woman looks

And sees the real you
Even through all the multiple women
And the blatant cheating and sinning
She sees your pain
Sees your past
Sees your scars
She just sees
You
don't need to use these super powers
In her heart is a home

Who knew
everything you was looking for
was formed in her
Times passes
A love story is told
A true bond unfolds
A little girl
is presented to the world
In 1991
You think this is it
the pain and abandonment is finally undone
But then she's taken from you and her
mum/

The Therapist's voice is bleeding through.

Distortion and glitching in the void. The Angel is aware of what's happening. It's breaking down around her. Mirrors are cracking slightly and The Angel is uncomfortable with the distortion. The void is getting more erratic.

Glitches are getting stronger and stronger.

The Angel disappears in a snap and Connor appears in her place at the microphone. Confused.

THE THERAPIST Please Connor take a seat

Another line of poetry bleeds through. Recited by Connor.

(V.O) **I pray to the lord for a drought**
Cos I cried so many tears I just want out
Standing at the feet
Of this giant beast called grief

WHAT DO I SEE?

THE THERAPIST *(V.O)* The date is Monday 16th January 2023.

I'm sat here with Connor.

Following on from our last session.

We are just going to explore further the issues raised about Blackness and absence.

So where shall we start...

Who showed you how to be a man?

CONNOR   Damn. That's tricky.

Like what does it even mean to be a man?

I guess

I would say my next door neighbour Jodi.

THE THERAPIST   Okay. In what ways did he show you how to be a man?

CONNOR   By giving me his time and that. Teaching me to shave, having my first pint with me/

THE THERAPIST   /And that what makes a man? Time, shaving, and pints?

CONNOR   When you put it like that, it seems stupid.

THE THERAPIST   Not in the slightest. It's what you associate with masculinity.

CONNOR   Always said anyone can be a father, but it takes someone special to be a dad.

Jodi's my dad. Gave me his time. Showed me love.

THE THERAPIST   And that's a man?

CONNOR   To me yeah.

To show love to a child that isn't even your own.

THE THERAPIST Do you think your father was shown love as a child?

CONNOR Dunno. Don't care! Don't matter what happened to you shouldn't beat your child with a belt. That's not love.

THE THERAPIST Well, Generational Trauma is passed down.

Inherently from one generation to the next be it through stories or actions.

CONNOR Isn't that like a buzz word though that people just use now.

Generational trauma.

THE THERAPIST In what way?

CONNOR I feel like I hear it all the time. Especially when I talk with my black friends and family.

It's always this generational bullshit of past ancestors.

THE THERAPIST How so?

CONNOR It always gets brought up.

Generational trauma.

Generational cycles. I'm like right... Okay.

THE THERAPIST Well dissect the word. You love words.

Generational trauma.

Trauma that's passed from generation to generation. Has nothing to do with skin colour or background. It's the trauma one has experienced and the effects of that trauma trickling down.

CONNOR   Right...

THE THERAPIST So not all trauma is race related.

CONNOR   But I can only go off personal experience.

Like for half my family it would be race related. So where do I sit in that?

THE THERAPIST Okay

But was your father absent because he was black? Or was he absent because he was human?

Pause.

The legacy of slavery is trauma. Passed down from generation to generation.

The void erupts and shakes a little.

CONNOR   Fuck!

THE THERAPIST Not often you're speechless.

The belt, physical punishment.

It's all interlinked.

Have you heard of the Willie Lynch Letter?

CONNOR   No.

THE THERAPIST Let me Rewind to 1700s.

Willie Lynch was a British slave owner who travelled to America. Gave a speech to other owners about how to ensure they have generations of slaves.

He focused on control by exploiting differences – light skin slaves would work in the house and do lighter jobs, dark skin slaves would be on a field doing hard labour.

Causes division.

> You would break in a horse so you do the same with a slave. Believing that by breaking their will, they would pass on that submissiveness to their offspring and so forth.
>
> It's not just the physical violence that keeps slaves in check, but the psychological manipulation too.

CONNOR You have wise words. I'll give you that.

THE THERAPIST You're the artist Connor. Not me.

Connor laughs.

> So colourism still exists and people don't see you as black or white or whatever. They see half of you as you put it.

CONNOR It's why I'm so scared of going to Jamaica.

They'll never accept me.

THE THERAPIST How do you know they won't accept you?

CONNOR Because they don't accept me here.

THE THERAPIST How are you not accepted?

CONNOR Things people say.

THE THERAPIST And what do people say?

Connor looks in the mirror and sees his father looking back.

CONNOR That I'm the right shade of Black.

That I'm palatable.

That I only have my success because I'm the right shade of Black. Whatever that even means.

Pause.

CONNOR   Sometimes I think... Do I endure pain as a way of punishing myself for what I did to my mum?

THE THERAPIST   Elaborate on that.

CONNOR   Well this success that I'm finding in my career I feel guilty for.

With George Floyd and what it's brought up.

Feels like organisations are using me and others as a tick box for diversity when I'm the lightest person in most rooms.

Like I don't deserve it.

Lucy interjects lurking in the void. Possibly talking straight to the audience.

LUCY   No need to thank me for the success I've given you.

Ungrateful little shit.

I've paved the path he is on and this is the thanks I get.

Can cover up his pain through work and accolades and all I get is a whiny little bitch in a therapy chair.

He's right. He is nothing like his father. His father had the balls to accept my deal and fuck the pain.

What a disappointment you are.

Lucy vanishes and the scene resumes.

CONNOR   All the mistakes I've made. All the hurt I've caused.

I slowly don't know who I am any more.

THE THERAPIST   That's an excellent and honest start. Continue.

Electic Riddim starts to play. Connor starts to spit into the microphone as the mic is his therapist. Here he is, fully raw and vulnerable.

CONNOR   What do I see

I see the biggest hypocrite in 2023

That's what I see. That's what I see

Listen to this story I'm sure you will agree

That's what I see

I see history playing out in the chapters of me

That's what I see

I see the apple.

It didn't fall far from the tree

That's what I see

I see Adam and Eve in the garden of Eden

Wanting knowledge to feed them

I see the chains they're wrapped around me

They're never setting me free

I see man whose face and features do pretty much resemble me

I see my fathers face when I look in the mirror and I look at my face

If my heart is a home and I'm sat all alone

And I screaming fuck this place

FUCK THIS PLACE

I see superpowers like charm and charisma
I see my fathers reflection
I'm like damn do I miss ya
Yeah, damn do I miss ya
I see a fractured soul who doesn't wanna admit
That he's still effected from this shit
Of an absent father
That's what I see.
That's what I see
I see my daddy issues
I see tears
I see kleenex tissues I see anger and rage
I see a child abandoned from a young age

I see a child who hates goodbyes
I see exactly how time flies

I see priorities misplaced
Now all I see is hate
I see a man who numbs his pain
Through money and sexual gain
Then acts like nothing aint changed
That's what I see
That's what I see

Am I my fathers son? or
Am I just like my mum?
I see them both

It's stunting my growth

That's what I see

THE THERAPIST So taking all that into consideration. You see an absence is that fair to say...? Something that's missing?

Do you see your father in some aspects

Pause.

CONNOR   I do. And I hate that.

THE THERAPIST He makes up 50% of your DNA. There's nothing to hate about that. We're all human beings. With joys and insecurities. We're flawed individuals.

In your father's case, it would be the question of what was missing for him? Only he can answer that.

But the same goes for you? What are you missing?

In your heart?

Connor leaves therapy through the mirror. He is back in the void looking at the different mirrors and memories.

THE THERAPIST I think you know what's missing.

I think you know where you have to go.

CONNOR   But I'm scared.

THE THERAPIST Fear has two meanings, Con.

Forget Everything And Run.

Or Face Everything And Rise.

JAMAICA

Sounds of an airplane taking off consume the void.

Connor and The Angel walk through the mirror to Kingston airport. They are greeted by a local.

Jamaican steel drums are playing.

LOCAL   Yuh there.

CONNOR   Yeah.

LOCAL   Weh yuh from?

CONNOR   UK. Wales.

Next to England.

LOCAL   Mi kno weh Wales is.

CONNOR   Oh my bad.

LOCAL   Yuh luk like yuh get a likkle sup'm inna yuh.

CONNOR   Oh! Yeah my father's Jamaican. From St Elizabeth.

LOCAL   What! Yaah sainty?

CONNOR   I mean my father is.

LOCAL   Nah yaah pickney of Jamaica.

You a child of Jamaica. Welcome home.

CONNOR   And just like that 30 years of fear and pain was evaporated.

The more I travelled this tiny island in the sea.

The more I got
Accepted just for me.

Something surreal happened.

Traveling the island with my driver, Raymond.

We went to St Elizabeth to see the old hardware store that my family used to own.

We ate some fried fish and a bammy on the side of a road

And listened to the stories from the elders as they got told.

The world is small.

On the other side of the planet.

I meet up with

Chantelle from an organisation back in Wales.

She takes me into a school.

And tells the kids that this man is half Jamaica.

Their eyes light up as I proceed to tell them.

They are all enough.

We create a poem.

Some creative stuff.

But as I spend time in the school it becomes clear that the level of poverty and deprivation is huge. Kids getting their only meal at this school.

Feeling so angry.

As the reality of this island hits me.

The local Jamaicans are banned from in order to make tourists feel safe. Their own land and they can't walk along her back.

This island that housed my father, my Gran, my ancestors. This paradise, I thought it was, has shown me the brutal reality that's far from funny.

Local women are selling themselves to American men for small amounts of money.

The reality I see forms a knot in my chest trying my absolute best.

To find water. To find rejuvenation.

There's wealth to this island no doubt, but it goes way beyond money.

They're rich in spirit and rich life.

A soundscape of all the people Connor met in Jamaica play out.

"You're a child of Jamaica, welcome home."

"Today was a blessing. Me opened my eyes. It's a blessing."

"Praise Jah. Life is good."

"Life is love ... Discover it."

"Life is a journey ... complete it."

Strings start to play out like the beat of a heart playing musically. (Little Simz – Blue instrumental)

ANGEL'S CRY

She wraps her arms around Connor like she's cradling a baby and he floats in the ocean.

This is the Angel's cry. A lullaby to accompany Connor throughout.

CONNOR   Thoughts of this island run through my mind.

Some are just cruel and some are just kind.

A combination of both

Thinking to myself, maybe it'll get better or maybe it won't

A third world country to some

Another missed call from my mum

So much pride and love oozes from every person I meet

Made me reflect, made me look in the mirror and know that my story is still incomplete

I swim out far, swim through the waves

The Angel floats with Connor. Together under the stars.

Searching for answers

floating on my back

Trying to find some peace from the constant battle

My heart and mind is under attack

I give myself to the water.

Floating the surface of the ocean's face

I give myself to the salt

Trying to understand that it was never my
fault
Cos I was just a child

Wondering if all my tears could fill the
ocean.
The pain carried from life to life
The scars have set my heart in motion
Never quite sitting right

Suffering in silence
Looking up at the stars for some guidance
For a sign
A piece of something that might be mine

Just floating

Nothing is present
Not even the time

There they all are
The stars
The ancestors

looking down from the ancestral plain
The gravity of so much generational pain
Pieces of my soul pieces of my heart
That all comes at a cost
All shining down

> The ones I've loved the ones I've lost

Colours start to immerse around the void. An amalgamation of purple and orange.

> I'm floating, I look out to the horizon.
>
> No one else in the entire ocean but me.
>
> Metamorphosis.
>
> Figuring out the Connor that I actually want to be.
>
> Who is he?
>
> Watching the middle of a lightning storm.
>
> The orange and purple separating.
>
> I can see straight through to heavens as the electricity crackled in the sky above beams of light snapped figures in the sky.
>
> Reminding me that I am always enough
>
> even though there's chapters of a story that seemed so tough.
>
> There's angels reminding me there's diamonds in the rough.

> I made it here.
>
> This small island that carried so much of my pain.
>
> I made it here and from this day nothing will be the same. This tiny island that housed so much of my family tree. This home in the Caribbean that birthed the features of me.

The Angel finishes off the lullaby/cry.

THE ANGEL   No more tears

No more tears

> No more tears for you and me
> No more tears
> No more tears
> Now your soul is almost free

The Therapist's voice can be heard like a voice recording through a mirror calling out.

THE THERAPIST   The date is Monday 10th July 2023.

I'm sat here with Connor the traveller.

So where shall we start…

The sound of an airplane taking off is heard and Bashy's Black Boys starts to build in quietly in the background, like it is coming through headphones.

CONNOR   "Black Boys Black Boys
Yeah we're all black boys
And one day we're gonna be black men
And one day we might have black boys
and we gotta teach them to be black men"

I'm sat on the plane.
Headphones on.
Spotify on shuffle.
Songs playing one after the other.
And I'm singing along.
Bobbing my head.

Bashy wrote that song when he was 21.
And I remember being this 15-year-old kid.
Back in 07.

With all the questions and confusions about race.

Thinking where was my dad to teach me how to be a man.

He's a Black man who had a mixed race boy.

But where was he to teach me how to be a man?

One day I might have a little boy and I'll have to teach him to be a man.

A cycle repeated over time.

And tears fill my eyes as I'm transported back to 07.

With that song, those lyrics and the chorus.

The Chorus plays out in the void.

"Ooh child, things are gonna get easier
Ooh child, things will get brighter"

And all I remember thinking is when are things gunna get easier?
When will they get brighter?

And honestly, I'm sat on this plane having spent 2 weeks in Jamaica.

With everyone being so friendly and loving and for the first time in my 3 decades.

It feels like it's getting easier.

The Angel appears and holds Connor as she sings to him.

THE ANGEL "Ooh child, things are gonna get easier
Ooh child, things will get brighter"

FATHER TIME

THE THERAPIST   How are you feeling after the trip?

CONNOR   Conflicted. If that makes any sense.

I felt more at home on that tiny island than I ever have done here in the UK.

Connor looks at the mirror.

It's hard learning to forgive myself for what I did to mum means like I'm growing init, but I'm not ready to forgive my father.

The anger and drive I had has been a part of who I am. But I don't know who I am without that anger.

The pain was something I wanted to hold onto.

As it made me who I am.

Forged me as I grew.

THE THERAPIST   Maybe it's time you let it go and started new.

Have you ever heard of Kintsugi?

CONNOR   No.

THE THERAPIST   Japanese. It's an art form where you put broken pottery pieces back together with gold. Building on the notion that by embracing flaws and imperfections you make a more beautiful piece of art.

Your guilt is a part of you. Embrace it and make more beautiful art.

CONNOR   I feel you! That makes a whole lot of sense.

Speaking of beautiful art.

I was listening to music on the flight.

And there was two songs.

One that I completely forgot about.

THE THERAPIST You do love a good song.

What was it?

CONNOR   Bashy's Black Boys.

It proper took me back.

THE THERAPIST I know the one.

CONNOR   You know Bashy's Black Boys?

THE THERAPIST I'm not a fossil, Con. Man knows good music.

They laugh.

What was the other?

CONNOR   Kendrick's 'Father Time'.

I can't lie, it messed me up.

It's beautiful. Kendrick raps about his dad and, although he was tough, he taught him everything he knows today. I was like my dad taught me fuck all

THE THERAPIST In what way?

Connor starts to spit into the microphone as Swiss Cry instrumental starts to play. The mic is his therapist. Here he is fully raw and vulnerable.

CONNOR   On repeat is Kendrick's Father Time

It's got me reflecting

On what I never got from mine

Got me lying to myself saying that I'm fine

When I'm not

I'm angry

All I ever wanted was a nuclear family

Mum and dad, little bro and me
I believed that would set my soul free
Install qualities in me
whilst you read me a bedtime story
With some clever metaphor about identity
And be a best friend to me
Like Woody was to Buzz in Toy Story
But that was never you
Man you had no clue
How to coach me
Through the things that I was going through

Needed assistance with my upbringing
Squash the demons in my head
That were stuck inging

But what have you given me
Honestly
Just some insecurity
About who I am
Where was you to teach me how to be a man?

It gets me angry
It gets me vexed
That you can't just pick up the phone
Send a text

Like how are you
What you up to son?

Where was you to pick me up and say I
love you son?

What have you instilled in me?
Nothing
What have you built for me?
Nothing
What have you gave me?
No love

No guarantee

It's crazy

It's just nothing

THE THERAPIST Ok, that's understandable.
There's an anger there still, but...
Could we flip the coin to the other side and
argue he gave you the greatest gift?

CONNOR How?

THE THERAPIST Did he not give you the greatest
gift in revealing himself to you? As he
showed you everything you never want to
be.

The void erupts and shakes a little.

CONNOR FUCK! Stop doing this.

*A swarm of butterflies surround Connor as he leaves
therapy.*

SECOND CHANCE

The Angel adjusts some mirrors, takes the mic, and goes to the grave and sits.

The Tems-inspired instrumental fades in.

THE ANGEL   The loss of a daughter
Yeah it hits you hard
Three months old
It breaks your relationship apart
You blame yourself
Whilst the mother of that child is in therapy
You're out in the world
Screaming

You need revenge
You don't want the rawest parts of yourself
revealing
Fast forward
Months and months pass

You're out there on some mad fuckery
Mistresses upon mistresses
All to mask the pain
The smudge of their kisses remain

The one year anniversary fast approaches
Of the birth of your little girl that was taken
You drink some rum like a proper Jamaican
One or two bottles later

You're knocking at the door
of your daughter's other creator

See who knew
After all that time the connection
A thread
Can't be broken
You're linked through loss

you can't be a liar
She sees right through
There's still a fire
A passion
So you kiss and kiss some more
She closes the front door
Pours a glass of wine

Then fast forward
9 months later
1992
You get the news
That a baby's been born
But now you're torn
Because you could lose him too
Who knew
You'd be scared
When you held your little boy
Looked into his hazel eyes and realised

Connor wasn't her

He wasn't your little girl/

The void starts to glitch causing The Angel to slowly disappear.

Another line of poetry bleeds through. Recited by Connor as he is seen in the mirror.

(V.O)   **I took time to walk through trauma's door**

unpacked my scars of before.

And I came to the realisation...

Connor fades.

Glitch.

A voice note from Blade bleeds through.

BLADE   Yo bro I know you are probably busy and all, but give mum a ring as she's blowing up my phone now.

Says she's been trying to get hold of you for time.

I told her you're probably busy and you're a fully grown man but you know what she's like, flapping as she can't get hold of you.

So yeah.

Ring her. Or else.... JOKES!

I mean not jokes. Actually ring her but jokes with the threats.

Love you.

You little bitch.

WHO AM I: THE LIGHT AT THE END OF THE TUNNEL

Connor looks in the mirror and sees nothing so punches it, smashing it which startles The Angel.

She sweeps up the glass as Connor is in the void looking at the other mirrors. He can't see his father.

Kendrick's 'Father Time' is playing in the background.

CONNOR There's something always weird about the post therapy feeling

That you understand or recognise part of the old you is leaving

So I stroll out the building

Just after 7

Look up to the heavens

Rains pouring down

I glance down at my phone

Missed call from mum

So I jump in the car

Ain't gotta travel too far

But who's this?

Lights all bright

Swerving all over the place.

The light catches up. A loud crash can be heard. Shattering the void.

COMPLETE BLACKNESS.

Seeing Green instrumental starts to be built layer by layer as the next scene happens.

SPINNING

Time has frozen and The Angel has confronted God to bargain with him.

THE ANGEL   Heavenly Father

Hear my pray

Please
Don't let this be it
There's still good in him
I know it
I have seen it

I haven't asked for much
in the 33 years i've been here
Just give me a chance
To help him make amends with his pain and regret
Because that world down there
It isn't done with him yet

Beat.

LUCY   He won't answer your prayer you know.

THE ANGEL   Lucy.

LUCY   That's his MO. False promises.

Casting his children out.
I remember the closeness I once had with him.
That father of mine.

THE ANGEL   What are you doing here?

LUCY   Same thing as you.

Here for Connor's soul.

THE ANGEL   Back off!

LUCY   Oh there's that feistiness I love so much. Such a shame you didn't join my rebellion down there.

THE ANGEL   I mean it Lucy. He's off limits.

LUCY   Far from it. If anything he's on limits.

Someone like Connor. Could serve me for decades.

You're not going to save him are you.

You've had years and failed.

Just staying on the sidelines for years watching from afar.

Like a coward.

THE ANGEL   You have no idea what you're talking about.

LUCY   I mean I know your little secret.

I know who you really are.

Beat.

I'll make you a deal.

You want him to live?

You can speak to him.

Talk him round.

Walk a different path.

The path of forgiveness

which we both know he'll never do.

So consumed with anger.

But then he'll have a choice.

If he rejects my offer then you are both free.

If he accepts it then I get his soul... and yours.

THE ANGEL   I know what you're doing.

LUCY   Hey, if you're so certain he'll find what he's looking for, then bet.

THE ANGEL   It's not as easy as/

LUCY   /Time's ticking away. Grim reaper is getting closer.

THE ANGEL   OK! Deal.

They shake hands and time unfreezes.

Seeing Green instrumental is built and The Angel joins in with the melody.

CONNOR   And time just slows down
to the point it freezes completely
well momentarily
Everything's becoming a blur
Moving so slow like I'm a speedster
traveling in flashtime
milliseconds upon milliseconds
is how it feels
As everything is spinning and spinning
And I'm losing control
Impact

     just spinning and spinning
with no idea of what to do
     No idea of what's gunna happen
I haven't got a clue
30 years
     flash
     Just like that

I see
the entire history

of me
play out in that moment
Like flicking
through 30 chapters
I never got my happy ever after
There's deep Regret
Acting out at childhood needs   that were never met

Shrapnel of alloy wheels
Dis
    in
        te
            gra
                ting
                    crumbling in the road
        Just asking is THIS
                        there where my story
            Finally stops getting told

        Parts of the car
            Detaching
                Flying out far
                    As I'm spinning
            and spinning
                And spinning
And

So many thoughts
So many unanswered questions
In that moment
Looking at past decisions
Future plans
I never got to complete my missions

my **purpose**
whatever that may be

Regret
I may not get the chance to grow older
Cos the grim reaper's there
He's lurking
Got his hands on my shoulder

So   the end is near
and within me
I have no fear
There's tranquility

Weirdly

Because
Maybe with my last breath I can finally have some rest

I'm at some sort of peace
From the dark thoughts in my mind
but the only thought I have is
I don't want mum to pick up the phone

Miss Allen your son is deceased
And that'll be two children she's lost
Not just her   but my father too
And the truth is I have no clue
                  how to apologise
                                    for the pain I caused
            the mistakes I made
I'm lost

Before my eyes my whole life is flashing
As my car spins out from the crashing
My souls taking a bashing
                  from confronting my own mortality
But the reality Is this may be it
This really may be it

PURGATORY

Connor is in purgatory. Nothing but mirrors. Sea of his own thoughts and past life. Looking in the mirror and seeing nothing The Angel is lurking.

THE ANGEL   Con listen to me we don't have much time.

CONNOR   What is this!?

Where the fuck am I?

THE ANGEL   Listen!

CONNOR   Who are you?

THE ANGEL   That's not important.

Who's the man YOU see when you look in the mirror?

Connor looks in the mirror and sees nothing.

THE ANGEL   It won't be blank forever.

I promise you.

The mirrors start to close in on Connor. The voice of Blade plays out in purgatory.

BLADE   Bro, you don't inspire others by being perfect...

You inspire them by how you deal with your imperfections.

Remember that.

You inspire me always like a big brother should.

I love you bro.

CONNOR   Blade? Whats happening. Make it stop!

The mirrors move closer encasing him like a cocoon.

THE ANGEL   The mirror won't be blank. But you have to finally confront the fear you have.

Your imperfections have never been your weakness.

You have to seek the answers to your questions.

You've been running for 30 years. It's time to stop.

CONNOR   Yo, whats happening. Make it stop

THE ANGEL   Then look in the fucking mirror and really look.

CONNOR   Don't make me do this. Please.

I beg you.

He looks in the mirror and still he sees nothing. Is it a blank canvas or a nothingness void?

THE ANGEL　　Who's the man you see when you look in the mirror.

Who do you see Con?

Who is the man you want to be?

You decide.

But those masks you constantly wear won't hide.

Who you really are inside?

The mirrors closes in around Connor until he is fully enclosed in the cocoon. It has started. Transformation.

He is surrounded by versions of himself in his own head. Voices echoing out overlapping each other. Building and building a crescendo of Connor's most rawest questions.

WHO AM I?

CONNOR　　What if I'm broken?

So damaged I can't be fixed

　　　　What if I'm scared to look in the mirror

　　　　　All I see is a wounded reflection

What if I'm terrified of happiness

As I'm so content with pain.

　　　　What if I'm never appreciative of time

　　　Spinning outta control as I leave 29

　　　　　What if I'm scared of being alone

　　　　　As I'm so used to being on my own

What if I'm self destructive
My worst fear is I'm just like my dad

She touches the cocoon. As she does this the cocoon is active and metamorphosis is happening.

This happens for a short time until the sound of a phone rings. It rings and rings then goes to voicemail, but this time the voicemail plays out.

MUM   Hey Con. It's Mum,

When you get a chance can you ring me please.

It's sort of urgent. It's about your father.

Thanks.

The Angel stands over the Grave. The Tems-inspired instrumental kicks in and she approaches the microphone.

THE ANGEL   Fast forward

Years and years go by

Your little son grows

Questioning why?

He got his little afro curls

But there's an absence that shows

In his heart when he thinks about his dad

But a cycle is continuing

When you don't show up

He starts to develop this exoskeleton

That's hardened and tough

Asking the same question as you did

On that beach

Why aren't I enough?

The questions
The insecurities
They stick with him as he enters puberty
But now he's rageful and bitter
At you
No clue
that you're just scared
Of losing him like you lost his sister
Damn you miss her

But now you're
Just watching your son's life in the
background
It makes him angry
That you're not around
He's like a ticking time bomb
Waiting to explode
The destructive path he is on
Has only one outcome
Another abandoned son

As he gets in more trouble with the police
He needs his dad, but it's your belief
That you never had yours so he doesn't
need his
Deep down
You want to show up and make him see

That you really do
But the reality hits And you remain

scared

Connor emerges. The void has transformed. It's Kintsugi.
Connor kneels by the hole and cries.

CONNOR   How can you welcome stability?
When all you've known is chaos
Like a wounded child
In an adult body

Who's the man you see when you look in
the mirror?

I used to see my father. Staring back
And I hated that
But the reality is
He is me and I am him

Lord forgive me for all my sins
I don't know if I believe in God
But I believe in external forces

And those forces are strong
Helping me write my wrongs
Confront my pain
To survive and live out a better day
One where there's colour in my grey

Cos I deserve to be free

From the weight
From the shackles

I finally see

me

Lucy appears.

LUCY   Now. You've been a very bad boy Connor.
You being here puts us in a predicament.
Please, sit.

He sits opposite Lucy.

See, many years ago
Your father made a family deal with me.
Signed a contract.
Power over women for his soul to cover up his wounds and it's been a very lucrative deal on my end.

And you sir were meant to carry that on.
I offered you the same deal.
As I see your anger.
Your disregard to other people's feelings.

I've been inside your head Connor.
Connor Allen.

The man who keeps running because he dare not look back at his past out of guilt and shame.

This is my everlasting victory.

I have shown you not only the man you hate.

But I have shown you, yourself.

Pause.

CONNOR You're wrong. Yeah I am like him. He's my father. But it's the choices we make that define us.

Beat.

You've seen my best and worst parts.

But I'm doing the work on me.

And your puppet is not the man I wanna be

Connor rips up the contract.

He grabs some chalk and draws a cross over the mirror to signal the end of the nine night. Lucy disappears as she has lost and her powers are depleted.

The void starts to break down and mirrors start to shatter and crack. His phone rings and he answers it.

CONNOR Hello.

MUM Hi did you get my voicemail?

CONNOR Yeah, been busy.

MUM Well it's your father, he wants to speak to you.

CONNOR About what?

MUM That's for him to tell you.

Connor stares at the only remaining mirror and walks through. He is in his father's living room with an elderly man. They have been there for a while.

FATHER Hi, please sit down.

FORGIVENESS / KUMINA

A rewind happens of all The Angel's story like we are going right back to the beginning. A reveal of the conversation Connor is having with his father. Instrumental of Bashy's Black Boys plays out.

CONNOR   I have proper been thinking these last few years

The love was there

The love was great

But my anger made me do things you hate

But the two of you look at this

Child that you make

This man who's grown

This man who's made some mistakes

Did I make you proud?

So how do I sum this all up

When all I had

Was a mother's love

But I guess

That was never enough

See

this is what dying does

I can't build any relationship without the trust

And

Deep down I don't wanna lose either one of us

A mother and a father

My creators

I pray to the lord for a drought
Cos I've cried so many tears I just want
out
When I'm standing at the feet
Of this giant beast called grief

You look at me
With those frail brown eyes
And a little walker beside. It's mad to think
I used to look at you like a king
Well actually a God
But what are the odds
That you ain't that no more

I took time to walk through traumas door
Unpack my scars of before
I came to the realisation
I don't want you anymore
You're just flesh and bones
A mortal man
Flawed and imperfect
With a story and a past
But that just makes you human

See
I can't hate you without hating me
Like Loyle Carner once said

"You can't hate the roots of a tree
without hating the tree"

And I don't hate you.
Because you were abandoned too
I now understand you're flawed

So, I appreciate you telling me your story
of that little boy on
the beach
Cos I finally see me in you.
I really do. So all I have to say is

thank you.

Beat.

FATHER   Better my story comes from me than someone else.

CONNOR   I agree.

Beat.

I should probably go.

Father stands up frailly to say goodbye to Connor.

FATHER   I'm sorry, son.
For everything.

Pause.

May I have a hug?

Connor reluctantly gives his father a hug. His father whispers to him.

Please forgive me?

There's a moment of connection in the hug. They hold each other like father and son.

Connor eases away from his father. Pause.

CONNOR   I forgive you.

Because I finally understand you.

And everything that you been through.

FATHER   I love you.

Connor shakes his father's hand and leaves to go back into the void.

CONNOR   My Gran told me they were called nine nights were because it takes nine nights for the soul to leave the body and go through to the afterlife.

During this period you celebrate. It's not a time for mourning because there is no more suffering.

Many people don't even know the person.

Gran would say "it's equally for the living as much as it is for the dead". Hearing stories uplifts your spirit. We are all built on stories. We can learn from stories.

Even if they're about someone you never met.

Connor looks at the grave.

For years I've been trying to kill the monster.

But slowly been killing me.

Each drop of soil Connor put onto the grave represents what he is burying and leaving to rest. All the things he no longer wants are getting buried.

The physical scars are visible.
The mental are the ones you don't see.
Coming to the realisation.
My father's human.
He's just as damaged as me.

So today I bury all the pieces.
Put that version of me to rest.

Cos I don't want this pain.
I don't wanna hurt.

I dont want this guilt anymore.

So I set free my demons
all the souls that are slain
So I set free
My mum
all the confusion she renamed blame
So I set free
My little bro
from both our parents pain
So I set free
My father
From Lucy's twisted game

Finally I set free myself
From all the mistakes that I made

THE ANGEL   Finally my work is done.

Now your soul is saved.

The Angel is watching on as Connor shovels the dirt back on the hole. He stops and looks in the mirror and sees himself for the first time.

You did it. I'm proud of you little bro.

You broke the generational curse.

Connor sees the butterfly in all its beauty and he smiles. He throws the shovel down and starts dancing Kumina.

It is healing. It is tribal. It is ceremonial.

The Angel joins him and they dance as brother and sister. Free from the pain They invite other to dance and drink. Freeing themselves.

The nine night is complete. And Connor's soul is free. They continue to dance and drink.

Lights fade down.

THE END.